Understanding Lutheran Worship

All rights reserved. Printed in the United States.

Second Edition, 2017
© 2016 St. John's Ev. Lutheran Church
Scripture quotations taken from NIV 1984

*For Pastor Steven Pagels and Pastor Joel Leyrer,
who inspired this book,
and for Pastor Kyle Bitter and Carolyn Sachs,
who helped bring it to fruition.*

Table of Contents

The Liturgy ■ 9

The Christian Church Year ■ 27

The Books of the Bible ■ 37

    Old Testament Biblical Notes ■ 39

    New Testament Biblical Notes ■ 54

References ■ 66

The Liturgy

The Liturgy ■

In his book *Letters to Malcolm,* the Christian writer and apologist C.S. Lewis compared the liturgy to a dance. "As long as you notice, and have to count, the steps, you are not yet dancing but only learning to dance . . . the perfect church service would be one we were almost unaware of; our attention would have been on God."[1]

The liturgy used in many Lutheran churches is also known as the *Divine Service.* It is a time when God serves his people by coming to them in Word and Sacrament. Worshipers then respond to these gifts by uniting their voices in prayer, praise, and thanksgiving. A deeper understanding of this interaction between God and his faithful people naturally leads to a more meaningful worship experience.

This compilation is designed to familiarize worshipers with the dance of the Lutheran liturgy. Through the following explanations of the liturgy, we hope and pray that you might better come to appreciate the beauty and simplicity of Lutheran liturgical worship. In the end, liturgical worship has a single focus: "The liturgy today does exactly what it did for Christians of ages past: it focuses the attention of worshipers squarely on the words and works of Jesus."[2] May you always keep this focus front and center as you dance the steps of the liturgy.

---

[1] C.S. Lewis, *Letters to Malcolm: Chiefly on Prayer* (San Diego: Harcourt, Inc., 1964), 4.
[2] Gary Baumler and Kermit Moldenhauer, ed, *Christian Worship: Manual* (Milwaukee: Northwestern Publishing House, 2002), 17

The Liturgy

Liturgy

Many Lutheran churches use a *liturgy* in their worship services. The word liturgy comes from two Greek words meaning "people" and "work." This style of worship, known as liturgical worship, is built on the historic Christian order of worship. "Lutheran respect for tradition shows a respect for ourselves as part of a greater community of saints . . . we are part of something larger than our local congregation or even our denomination. We are part of the Body of Christ"[3] Despite being centuries removed from the early Christian Church, the basic form and primary focus of worship—that is, the liturgical style—has remained constant.

God grants his people freedom in worshiping him, and therefore not all Lutheran churches elect to use a liturgy. Liturgical worship allows for great variety within a set pattern. It is not tied to a specific musical style, nor does it prefer one musical instrument over another. However, the liturgy used in the majority of Lutheran churches generally follows an orderly progression of thought focusing the worshiper on the means of grace.

The Lutheran liturgy contains a set pattern of basic elements such as canticles, Scripture readings, prayers, and hymns. Liturgy can also refer to different orders of worship. Common examples are Matins (Morning Praise), Divine Service (Common Service, Service of Word and Sacrament, Service of the Word), Vespers (Evening Prayer), Compline (Prayer at the Close of Day) and others. It does not always contain the same liturgical elements. Many of these liturgical elements are described in more detail in the following explanations.

Ultimately, the liturgy serves as a cradle for the means of grace. Through the liturgy, the Gospel is proclaimed, sins are forgiven, and the Sacraments are distributed. Through the liturgy, Jesus Christ is worshiped and proclaimed.

Ordinary and Proper

Most liturgical elements fall into one of two categories: ***ordinary or proper.*** Ordinary elements are portions of the service that do not change substantially from week to week. They may change form slightly, but the basic liturgical element remains the same. Examples of ordinaries include the invocation, confession and absolution, Kyrie, Gloria, salutation, creed, Lord's Prayer, and the canticles sung during the Sacrament.

Proper elements are portions of the service that vary according to the Sunday and season of the church year. Examples of propers include the hymns, prayer of the day, lessons, verse of the day, and the sermon.

---

[3] Timothy H. Maschke, *Gathered Guests: A Guide to Worship in the Lutheran Church* (St. Louis: Concordia Publishing House, 2009), 44.

The Liturgy

Cross Processional

Cross processionals have been a part of Christian worship since the 4th century. "During the 12th century, candles and a cross were regularly placed on altars. Prior to this time, candles and the cross were carried only during the entrance procession; then they were placed on stands . . . an ancient tradition of the Church forbade placing anything on the altar except that which was specifically needed for the celebration of Holy Communion."[4] In a cross processional, the cross and candles (historically known as torches) are carried into the sanctuary during the opening hymn. The processional cross reminds worshipers that the Christian Church follows Christ.

Opening Hymn

In present-day language, the word *hymn* is a generic term for any kind of song suitable for the congregation to sing in worship. As Lutheran Christians, our hymns are both a confession and a response to the gracious working of the triune God for us and in us. If the text of a hymn does not contain this message of salvation, there can be no strengthening of faith by its singing.[5]

The **opening hymn** is a touchpoint for gathering God's people together in worship. "Its purpose is to knit together and bring to a focus the thoughts of God's saints who have come from various places and backgrounds to worship the Lord . . . it is a sign that God has entered the place where the faithful are gathered in his name."[6] The opening hymn serves to unify the congregation as its members prepare to worship in the presence of God. It has historic roots in the Introit, a psalm chanted at the beginning of the service by the choir while the clergy entered the sanctuary. With this hymn, we announce boldly that God—Father, Son, and Holy Spirit—is here. Our Lord who loves to be worshiped is present among us.

Sacrament of Holy Baptism

Lutheran Christians attach a three-fold meaning to the word "sacrament": a sacred act 1) instituted by Christ; 2) that uses earthly elements connected with God's Word; 3) by which God offers, seals, or gives to us the forgiveness of sins. **Baptism** is one of the two sacred acts in the Bible that fulfills this definition.

In Matthew 28, Jesus commands baptism when he says, "Go and make disciples of all nations, baptizing them in the name of the Father and of the Son and of the Holy Spirit" (Matthew 28:19).

---

[4] Maschke, *Gathered Guests*, 232.
[5] Baumler and Moldenhauer, *Manual*, 230.
[6] Baumer and Moldenhauer, *Manual*, 169.

The Liturgy

Baptisms have been performed in the corporate worship service for several hundred years, but they have only been included with regularity in the corporate worship service over the last 75 years. "In earlier years, however, baptisms were often performed at the home of the parents or in a private service or in a separate building called the baptistery."[7] In the Sacrament of Holy Baptism, the Holy Spirit washes away sin and (in the case of infants) makes a little child God's child through the water and the Word. When that child is baptized, he/she also becomes a part of a Christian family.

Although baptism is performed only once, it should be an event that Christians remember and return to throughout their lives. Whenever a baptism is performed, it is an opportunity for all believers to rest secure in the new life in Christ they received through their own baptism. "We [rest] our confidence in the security of our baptism, which neither Satan nor sin can tear away from us."[8]

Baptism Affirmation

In Matthew 28, Jesus gives his Church the clear command to baptize, but nowhere in the Scriptures does God command the *affirmation of baptism.* So what purpose does this public rite serve? If a baby is baptized privately at home or in the hospital, the parents may choose to schedule an affirmation a few days or weeks later to give public testimony that their child has been baptized, to give thanks for God's blessings, and to give their Christian brothers and sisters the opportunity to welcome that child into the family of believers.

Invocation and Apostolic Blessing

Following the opening hymn, the service begins in one of two ways. Some versions of the Divine Service begin with the *invocation* (meaning "to call upon"). In the words of the invocation, the congregation is assured that the God they are worshiping is the true God: Father, Son, and Holy Spirit. The invocation also reminds worshipers of the words used in Holy Baptism—words by which they were adopted into the family of God and made members of his Church. "The invocation reminds us that only through faith can we come into God's house and approach God's heavenly throne. We invoke God only because we have been made one of God's gathered guests through the waters of Baptism."[9]

In other forms of the Divine Service, the pastor announces a *blessing* upon all who have gathered for worship. The greeting is called "apostolic" because the words are taken from the Apostle Paul's blessing at the end of 2 Corinthians (13:14). All three persons of the Trinity are included in this greeting. The pastor makes the sign of the cross as he speaks to emphasize the redeeming work of Jesus Christ. With the response, "And also with you," the worshipers extend the same greeting and blessing to the worship leader.

---

[7] Baumer and Moldenhauer, Manual, 165.
[8] Baumer and Moldenhauer, *Manual,* 166.
[9] Maschke, *Gathered Guests,* 138.

The Liturgy ■

Confession and Absolution

When we approach our holy Lord in worship, it is appropriate that we confess our sins to him and seek his forgiveness. Originally, corporate confession and absolution were not found in the historic liturgy. Church members confessed privately to the minister. Absolution was conferred verbally in private and corporately in the Sacrament of Holy Communion.

Over time, Christians recognized value in proclaiming sin and forgiveness publicly. Today, after the invocation or the dialogue of blessing, the minister leads the congregation into the **confession of sins**—the daily drowning of our sinful nature. In the **absolution,** the minister announces forgiveness to the penitent congregation, confidently appealing to the atoning sacrifice of Jesus Christ as the basis for forgiveness.[10] After hearing the Gospel words of forgiveness in the absolution, the congregation responds with a spoken amen. By speaking the *amen,* the congregation verbalizes its faith and expresses agreement with this good news of forgiveness and absolution.

Kyrie

Kyrie is the Greek word for *Lord.* The Kyrie ("Lord, have mercy") has been used as a response by the Christian Church since ancient times. It is the first of five major liturgical songs or *canticles.* A canticle (coming from the Latin for "little song") is a liturgical song based on a Biblical text, but not generally coming from the Psalms.[11]

In some forms of the Divine Service, the Kyrie is placed between the confession of sins and the absolution. It is sung as a penitential plea for forgiveness to the triune God.

In other Divine Service forms, the Kyrie is placed after the confession of sins and the absolution. In this context, the Kyrie is not a plea for forgiveness, because we have just received forgiveness in the absolution. In this forgiveness, worshipers boldly come before God and make requests, just as believers have always called for God's help and aid (see especially Matthew 15:22 and Mark 10:46-47). The words "Lord, have mercy" could also be expressed as "Lord, help us" or "Lord, hear our prayer." In the Kyrie we pray for the needs of ourselves, the Church, and the whole world. The Kyrie can be sung in confidence because we know that we have a merciful and loving God who comes to the aid of his people.

---

[10] Baumler and Moldenhauer, *Manual,* 170.
[11] Baumler and Moldenhauer, *Manual,* 153.

Gloria

The **Gloria** is the second of the five major liturgical canticles. The Gloria—a triumphant song of praise—takes different forms in the various versions of the Divine Service.

The Gloria begins with an echo of the angels' joyful proclamation the night of Jesus' birth: "Glory to God in the highest, and on earth peace to men on whom his favor rests" (Luke 2:14). On that night, their praise gave voice to the good news that the Son of God had come in the flesh. Ever since, the Church continues to rejoice in this miracle of our salvation. These opening words are followed by a hymn of praise, glory, and thanks to the triune God. The focus is on the incarnate Son of God, the one who is the object of our worship and praise: the only-begotten Son, the Lamb of God, the only Son of the Father. The *Gloria* encompasses the very heart and substance of the Christian faith when it proclaims Jesus to be the one who takes away the sin of the world. Luther said that this ancient song "did not grow, nor was it made, but it came from heaven."

At other times, we substitute a different canticle for the Gloria. In one of these, the congregation confidently responds to the announcement of forgiveness with the words of "O Lord, Our Lord," a song of glory, praise, and thanks to the triune God. This canticle of praise emphasizes believers' thanksgiving to God for all he has accomplished for us through Christ.

A third song of praise uses the words of Psalm 34:8 and 119:89-90, which are set to music in the canticle "Oh, Taste and See." This canticle was newly composed for *Christian Worship.* It praises the goodness of God and the firmness of his eternal Word. "Oh, Taste and See" and the other canticles used in *Christian Worship* provide an outlet of thanksgiving to God for all he has accomplished for us through Christ. We rejoice in the assurance that we are indeed forgiven children of God!

During the Easter season, the canticle "This is the Feast" is often used as a song of praise. The text of "This is the Feast" comes primarily from Revelation 5:12-13. It is particularly appropriate to sing it during the Easter season as we celebrate the victory of Christ the Lamb of God and look forward to his eternal heavenly reign. In singing "This is the Feast," there is no refrain between stanzas 3 and 4. This reinforces the words of stanza 4 as the "hymn of all creation" referenced in stanzas 3.

The Liturgy ■

Salutation

Along with the preface to the Sacrament of Holy Communion, the words of the *salutation* between the pastor and the congregation ("The Lord be with you."/ "And also with you.") are some of the oldest responses in the liturgy. They are reminiscent of greetings between believers found in Scripture, especially Ruth 2:4. The salutation anticipates what will come next in the service: the reading of the Scriptures, the sermon, and the creed—that is, hearing and confessing the Word of God.

Through the salutation, the pastor conveys his desire that God will be with his congregation and bless them as they hear the Word. Similarly, by their response the congregation recognizes that their pastor will be serving them by reading and preaching the Word. They desire a similar blessing for their pastor as he continues the important work of serving his congregation through the Word.

Prayer of the Day

The **Prayer of the Day** is a prayer that often focuses on the content of the Gospel or Second (Epistle) Lesson, aiding in the unity of thought throughout the service. This prayer is somewhat poetic and reverent in nature. Many of the Prayers of the Day have deep roots in the history of the Christian Church. We should be careful to avoid the mistaken notion that written prayers are not spiritual. On the contrary, a written prayer is a well thought out reflection of the God of order.

Christian Worship and *Christian Worship Supplement* Lectionary

A **lectionary** is the list of readings for a given Sunday or festival of the church year. Public reading of the Scriptures has always been an important part of worship. Two lessons were read in the Jewish synagogue: one from the law and one from the prophets. Along with these lessons, the early Christians also began to read from the Gospels and the letters of the apostles, now known as epistles.

The lectionary (series of readings) used by many Lutheran churches is based on a three-year cycle. For the most part, this lectionary corresponds to a series of readings developed in the early 1970s. The First Lesson comes from the Old Testament (except during the Easter season, when it is from Acts) and is generally chosen to match the emphasis of the Gospel. The First Lesson was added in the 1970s revision to the lectionary to better acquaint worshipers with Old Testament history. The Second Lesson comes from a New Testament epistle. On the Sundays after Pentecost, a running series of four to six readings from the same book is used. Each year, one of the Synoptic Gospels (Matthew, Mark, or Luke) serves as the basis for the Gospel, with readings from John used during the Easter season in all three years. A full listing of the three year lectionary lessons can be found on pgs. 163-165 of *Christian Worship*.

In addition, a new supplemental lectionary has been produced in conjunction with *Christian Worship Supplement*. The Gospel remains unchanged in the supplemental lectionary. However, many of the First Lessons have been revised. The *Christian Worship* lectionary is weighted heavily with readings from the Old Testament prophets. In their place, the supplemental lectionary proposes a significant number of narrative texts, or Bible stories, which connect thematically with the Gospel. Some of the Second Lessons have also been revised to provide an unmistakable connection with the Gospel. In addition, as much as possible, readings were chosen from every book of the Bible.

Psalm of the Day

Use of the ***psalms*** in worship dates back to the Old Testament, where the common recitation of the *Psalter* (book of psalms) served to unite the Jews scattered across the lands. The Psalter was the first hymnbook of the early Christians. The medieval church also chanted large portions of the Psalter in the liturgy of the Mass. "The psalms have long been one of the great poetic treasures of the Church. Their inspired content and their ability to lift people from the depths and restore faith, trust, and joy account for their favored place in the lives of Christians."[12] In singing the psalms as God's people have across the centuries, we proclaim the peace of Christ that dwells in us richly.

Verse of the Day

The ***Verse of the Day*** is a familiar or significant Scripture text, bookended with alleluias (which are omitted during the Lenten season). It is a *proper*—that is, it changes each Sunday. The Verse of the Day mirrors the Sunday, festival, or season of the church year. Its placement between the Second Lesson and the Gospel is designed to increase understanding of the lessons. It looks forward to and welcomes the reading of the Gospel. Some of the verses are from the Old Testament, but more come from the New Testament. A number of them are from one of the four Gospels.

---

[12] Baumler and Moldenhauer, *Manual*, 151.

The Liturgy

Gospel

The **Gospel** (Greek for *"good news"*) sets the theme for the entire worship service. It is a record of the very words and deeds of Jesus and is treated with reverence. The congregation stands for its reading. This tradition of standing serves as a visual reminder that the Gospels are the climax of the Scriptures. The rest of the Old and New Testaments center around who Jesus is and what he did for us as recorded in the Gospels. In the Gospels, we see the very events of Jesus' perfect life, innocent death, and resurrection—"the power of God that brings salvation; the old news that is always new and good."[13]

Gospel Acclamation

After hearing the words of Jesus in the Gospel, the congregation responds joyously with the **Gospel Acclamation:** "Praise be to you, O Christ." We praise our crucified and risen Lord whose words we heard in the Gospel and who fulfills all of God's Old and New Testament promises.

Anthem

The **anthem** is a more recent addition to the liturgy. Known as the "choir's sermon," it has its roots in Reformation era worship. Historically, the music was more elaborate and complex than hymn or psalm settings. In the 15th and 16th centuries, the anthem was often an extensive musical work, sometimes combined with the hymn of the day. Today, the anthem is generally chosen to reflect the theme of the service as seen through the Gospel.

Hymn of the Day

The **hymn of the day** is generally viewed as the "teaching" or "liturgical" hymn of the worship service. This hymn usually has the deepest theological text as compared to the rest of the hymns in the service. It is most closely connected to the Gospel and is specifically chosen to reinforce the congregation's understanding of the Gospel which was just read.

The hymn of the day has its roots in two parts of the historic liturgy: a psalm originally located between the Epistle Lesson and the Gospel, and later an extended choral piece known as a cantata that followed the Gospel. The hymn of the day is a distinctly Lutheran contribution to the liturgy designed to encourage congregational participation. Because the hymn of the day for each Sunday of the church year was selected by the Lutheran church in the 16th century, many of these hymns are Lutheran chorales.

---

[13] Baumler and Moldenhauer, *Manual,* 186.

Sermon

In the Jewish synagogues, commentary followed the readings. Therefore, the **sermon** has ancient historical roots. This concept of commentary carried over into the New Testament Church, where the sermon was a part of worship from the 1st century. Virtually every gathering of believers included discourses on or explanations of the lessons. By Luther's time, however, the sermon was rarely included in corporate worship. One of Luther's most important reforms was a restoration of the sermon with true gospel preaching on Biblical texts.

The sermon serves as the culmination of the service of the Word that began with the readings. The ultimate goal of the sermon, like the liturgy as a whole, is to serve the Gospel. "There are a number of things a sermon ought not to be, but there is one thing the sermon ought always to be: the Word of God, proclaiming the living voice of the Gospel to God's redeemed people."[14] The sermon seeks to instill in the congregation a deeper understanding of the truths contained in God's Word.

Creed

The word **creed** comes from the Latin word *credo*, which means "I believe." The three creeds that Lutherans confess regularly in their worship services— Apostles', Nicene, and Athanasian—are called *ecumenical* because they are accepted by many Christians throughout the world. These creeds are ancient, dating to the early years of the Christian Church. In confessing these ancient creeds, we remind ourselves that what we believe and teach has been handed down to us by the apostles and by Jesus himself. In addition, we do not confess these creeds alone. We are invisibly united with Christians across the centuries by a common faith, and we are encouraged by the timelessness of our confession in the creeds. The creed was originally chanted, making it the third of the five major liturgical canticles.

After listening to the sermon, the congregation confesses its faith in the triune God. In services without the Lord's Supper, the Apostles' Creed is used. The Apostles' Creed is a more personal confession, using the words "I believe . . ." as opposed to the "We believe . . ." of the Nicene Creed. The Apostles' Creed is so named not because it was written by Jesus' apostles, but because it is a brief statement of the gospel truths they taught. Its writing and use dates to the very early years of the Christian Church.

---

[14] Baumler and Moldenhauer, *Manual*, 156.

The Liturgy

The Nicene Creed is so named because it was developed at the Council of Nicaea in 325 AD. The Nicene Creed is a corporate confession of the Church in defense of the Bible's teaching on the triune God, with special emphasis given to the personhood of Jesus. While the opening words of the Apostles Creed ("I believe . . .") stress the personal nature of confession, the "We believe . . ." of the Nicene Creed emphasizes that Christians are united by a common faith and that our unity is founded on the timeless truth of God's Word. This unity of faith, along with the more detailed exposition of Jesus' dual nature (true God and true man), leads to the use of the Nicene Creed in services with Holy Communion.

The Athanasian Creed was written in the 4th century to assist the Church in combating two errors that undermined Bible teaching: the denial of the doctrine of the Trinity and the denial of the dual nature of Jesus Christ (true God and true man). Because of its emphasis and clear exposition of the triune God, it is often confessed on Trinity Sunday. The second half of the creed is a beautiful explanation of the doctrine of *Christology:* the study of the nature and person of Jesus.

Offering

The creed, **offering,** and Prayer of the Church can be viewed as the "fellowship" portion of the worship service where we celebrate our united participation in the church's mission. In these service elements, we confess our common faith, we band together and share our gifts to support the promotion of that faith, and we then pray for others who share that faith.

Crucial to Christian giving is the understanding that everything we have is God's. We are simply called to manage what God already owns. Our gifts and offerings are a response to the Lord for his goodness to us. They are to be given on a regular basis and should be the first fruits of what we receive.

Prayer of the Church

The **Prayer of the Church** might also be called the Prayer *for* the Church, since it is a fellowship prayer for all of God's people here on earth. In other words, this is a time of prayer on behalf of the Christian Church at large. We pray for those in our congregation, but we also pray for the needs and struggles of God's people around the world. In this prayer, we are again reminded that we are not only members of our congregation but also a part of the holy Christian and apostolic Church. We receive encouragement from the knowledge that we share a common faith with our brothers and sisters in Christ, and we remember them in our prayers.

The Liturgy

Lord's Prayer

The **Lord's Prayer** was given by Jesus in response to his disciples' request, "Lord, teach us to pray." This prayer is both one that we should pray often and one that should serve as a model for all our prayers. In this prayer, we pray to "Our Father in heaven," reminding us that we are God's chosen and dearly loved children and members of his family.

Sacrament of Holy Communion

Lutheran Christians attach a three-fold meaning to the word "sacrament": a sacred act 1) instituted by Christ; 2) that uses earthly elements connected with God's Word; 3) by which God offers, seals, or gives to us the forgiveness of sins. The Lord's Supper is one of two sacred acts in the Bible which fulfills this definition, which we are to do "often." Most Lutheran churches obey this command by celebrating the Lord's Supper every week or every other week, as well as on festival services throughout the church year.

In the **Sacrament of Holy Communion,** we receive Jesus' true body and blood which is present in, with, and under the bread and wine. We first celebrate the vertical relationship between God and his children. We are reminded of the gift of Jesus' redemption and proclaim his death until he comes again in glory. We also celebrate the horizontal relationship we share as a body of fellow Christians. By participating in the Lord's Supper, we bear witness to the fellowship and unity which is ours through our shared faith.

Preface

The **preface**—words of dialogue between the pastor and the congregation—are some of the oldest in the Christian liturgy, dating back to A.D. 200. They transition from the part of the service centered on the Word to the part centered on the meal that Christ instituted.

The first set of responses ("The Lord be with you." / "And also with you.") are the same as the salutation before the Prayer of the Day. They remind us that our Lord comes to us both in Word (earlier in the service) and Sacrament (upcoming in the service). The second set of responses ("Lift up your hearts." / "We lift them up to the Lord.") anticipates the rest, forgiveness, and uplifting we will receive in the Sacrament. The third set of responses ("Let us give thanks to the Lord our God." / "It is good and right so to do.") encourages thankfulness for the meal which we are about to receive. These words are reminiscent of a common Jewish prayer used before meals and of the account of the institution of the Lord's Supper, where Jesus "took the cup [and] gave thanks" (Matthew 26:27).

The Liturgy ■

Proper Preface

The thanksgiving called for in the preface continues in the ***proper preface***: a prayer thanking God for his various blessings offered through Christ. The proper preface includes a text specific to the current season of the church year. This text gives the congregation an opportunity to thank God for specific blessings appropriate to the season.

The conclusion of the proper preface reminds us that by partaking of Christ's body and blood, we are united with the whole Christian Church—those who have gone before us and those who will come after us. In this Sacrament, we are given a foretaste of the feast that is to come, the wedding supper of the Lamb which will never end.

Sanctus

The ***Sanctus*** (coming from the Latin word for "holy") is the fourth of the five major liturgical canticles. It begins with an echo of the song of the seraphim from Isaiah 6:3 and continues with the words of the crowds on Palm Sunday: "Hosanna in the highest!" These words, used centuries ago to greet the promised Messiah, remind us that Jesus also comes to us today in the Sacrament. He is the second person of the triune God, praised by the seraphim in Isaiah's vision.

Although the Church may be visibly separated by geography, language, custom, and time, in reality we are one body, united in Christ. "[Isaiah] describes the seraphim gathered around the throne of God, chanting a confession of God's supreme 'otherness' . . . we also are able to participate in this inspired adoration as our worship takes on a supertemporal nature…and becomes truly eternal." [15]

Prayer of Thanksgiving

In some versions of the Divine Service, the ***Prayer of Thanksgiving*** is part of the preparation for Holy Communion. While this element of the service is new to WELS congregations, it has a storied tradition in Church history. This prayer, usually called the Eucharistic Prayer, was eliminated by Martin Luther in his reform of the Mass because it had been corrupted to emphasize human action toward God rather than God's actions toward his people.

---

[15] Maschke, *Gathered Guests*, 166.

After discussion and study, the Prayer of Thanksgiving was re-written and re-introduced in *Christian Worship Supplement* as a natural conclusion to the call for thanks at the end of the preface. This prayer directs the congregation's attention towards what God does for his people, especially his work in the Sacrament. Although we bring the bread and wine, God is the one doing the feeding. Because of the unity we enjoy as brothers and sisters in faith, we are able to stand before the altar of God together and confess the foundation of our faith: the forgiveness of sins freely given to us through Jesus.

Words of Institution

In the **Words of Institution,** the pastor uses Christ's own words to consecrate—set apart—the bread and wine. These words "are not a magic formula that brings about a change in the elements."[16] But because they are the words of Jesus put into the minister's mouth, they still accomplish today what they accomplished on Maundy Thursday: effecting the real presence of Jesus' body and blood in, with, and under the bread and wine.

Pax Domini (Peace)

Following the Words of Institution, the pastor proclaims peace to the congregation through the **Pax Domini** (Latin for "peace of the Lord"). These words call to mind Jesus' greeting to his disciples locked in the upper room on Easter evening (John 20:19). In a sense, this is another point in the service where the worshipers receive absolution and assurance that God's presence and peace are with them through partaking of the Sacrament.

The congregation responds to the pastor's words by speaking or singing "amen." "In Christ all things are ready. Now it is time to come to the altar of the Lord."[17]

Agnus Dei

The **Agnus Dei** is the last of the five major liturgical canticles. Its Latin title simply means "Lamb of God." Believers approach the altar of God by the sacrificial substitute who died in our place. We join with the cry of John the Baptist to the Lamb who takes away the sin of the world (John 1:29) and grants us mercy and peace. The Christian Church has sung this text before communion for more than thirteen centuries. The three-fold repetition draws our attention to the triune nature of God.

---

[16] Baumler and Moldenhauer, *Manual*, 177.
[17] Baumler and Moldenhauer, *Manual*, 190.

Distribution Hymns

During the distribution of the Lord's Supper, **distribution hymns** may be sung. These hymns are usually chosen according to one of two emphases: reinforcement of the theme of the day or a focus on Holy Communion. Hymns chosen to reinforce the theme of the day remind worshipers of the message proclaimed in the readings and further expounded upon in the sermon. A hymn of this type is designed to imprint this message on the worshipers' minds by setting it to music. Hymns chosen to focus on Holy Communion remind worshipers of the blessings they receive from God through the distribution of the Sacrament. By singing these hymns, worshipers in turn proclaim these blessings and the peace that accompanies them to one another.

Nunc Dimittis

The congregation responds to the Sacrament by singing the **Nunc Dimittis.** Latin for "now dismiss," these are Simeon's words from Luke 2:25-35 as he held the baby Jesus in the temple. The Greek used by Simeon suggests the idea of a soldier or sentry being relieved of his post, or that of a slave being ordered on to a different mission now that his current mission is completed. Simeon had completed his mission of waiting for the Messiah and was ready to proclaim what he had seen.

This canticle was historically sung during the evening services of Vespers and Compline. It is a fitting addition to the post-communion liturgy as we close the service by thanking our God for the gifts and forgiveness offered in the Sacrament. When we sing Simeon's words we are reminded that in the Sacrament, we too have seen the Lord's salvation. Having seen this salvation, we are ready to depart from the church building in peace and to live for God by proclaiming what we have seen to the world around us.

Post-Communion Prayer

Following the Nunc Dimittis and prior to blessing the congregation, the pastor offers a **prayer of thanksgiving** for the gifts received in the Sacrament. Through these words, we offer thanks for the forgiveness of sins, strengthening of faith, and spiritual refreshment offered through Holy Communion. The Communion liturgy ends in the same way it began—by offering thanks and praise to God.

Aaronic Blessing

The blessing spoken by the pastor at the close of the service is known as the **Aaronic blessing.** These words were first given to Aaron and his sons (the priests) by the LORD and were used to bless the people of Israel (Numbers 6:22-27). Just as we began the service in the name of the triune God, so we also end the service in his name. The blessing is God's assurance that he will go with us as we leave the church and return to the world to serve him. We sing or speak "amen" to affirm the blessing—"so be it, it is true!"

Closing Hymn

With the **closing hymn,** the worship service is ended. This hymn is chosen to help worshipers take the message or theme of the day home with them. Often it will be a familiar hymn that resonates beyond the worship service. In this hymn, the congregation reaffirms and proclaims the truths that have been shared throughout the entire service. After the hymn, the worshipers go out in peace to live in fellowship with one another, to encourage each other, and to be God's salt and light to the world.

Standing, Sitting, and Kneeling

To those unfamiliar with liturgical worship, the directions for sitting, standing, and kneeling may seem arbitrary and confusing. But each posture conveys a specific message and is done for an intentional reason in the worship service.

We **stand** out of respect for our Lord and his Word. This is seen most notably in standing for prayer and for the reading of the Gospel—the very words of Jesus. We also stand to confess our faith in the creed. We **sit** to be instructed: for the sermon and the other Scripture lessons. Most congregations today also sit for the hymns, mainly out of consideration for worshipers who are unable to stand for longer periods of time. In the early Christian Church, however, the believers stood to sing praises to their God. We **kneel** before God our King when we are in his presence: specifically, when we ask him to forgive us in the confession of sins. At some churches, worshipers will also kneel for communion, where they receive the very body and blood of the Lord.

The Christian Church Year

The Christian Church Year

Our lives are shaped and structured by time. Throughout the course of our lives, we mark hours, days, weeks, months, and years—and sometimes even minutes and seconds. Time establishes a rhythm for our lives, and how we use our time demonstrates what is most important to us.

This same principle applies to Christian worship. Instead of trying to escape time, the early Christian Church used time to structure its worship. Over the centuries, this focus developed into what we now know as the church year.

Although using the church year is not a requirement for being a Christian church, many Christian churches choose to structure their calendar and worship around the church year. They do so because the church year is an incredible gift from the early Christian Church to future generations. It gives us a structure for remembering God's magnificent acts in time—in the past, in the present, and in time yet to come. Instead of trying to escape time, Christian worship uses time to tell and mark the story of God's salvation.

In conjunction with the church year, Christians also use color in worship. The color designated for a Sunday or festival calls attention to the season of the church year and establishes the appropriate mood for that season. These colors can be seen in the altar cloths (paraments), the pastors' stoles (vestments), and often in banners or other church accessories.

Through the following explanations of the various festivals and seasons of the church year, we hope and pray that you might better come to appreciate the church year's structure and rhythm. In the end, the church year centers around the life and teaching of our Savior. May you always keep this focus front and center as you move through the timeline of your life.

The Christian Church Year

Advent

Advent is a Latin word that means "coming." The season of Advent consists of the four Sundays before Christmas. This is the season of the church year when we celebrate the coming of Christ. He came once as a baby in Bethlehem. He comes to us today in his Word and through the Sacraments. And he will come again in glory at the end of time.

On each of the four Sundays in Advent, a new candle is lit on the Advent wreath. The general symbolism of the Advent wreath lies in the growing light of the candles. This light dispels the darkness as the Church moves toward Christmas when it will welcome Jesus, the One who is the true light of the world.

The liturgical color for Advent used to be purple, the color of royalty, in honor of Christ the coming King. But for most churches today, the color is **blue,** perhaps to set Advent apart from Lent. Blue is the color of hope and the color of the sky. We are reminded that it is from the sky that Jesus will come again to take us to be with him forever, and this fills us with a sure and confident hope.

Christmas

Christmas comes from the Old English words *Cristes moesse,* "the mass or festival of Christ." The historical reason for observing Christmas on December 25 is not certain. One theory states that this date was chosen to provide a Christian counterpoint to the pagan Roman festival celebrating the sun god. Another theory puts Christmas exactly nine months after March 25, the vernal equinox. The Annunciation was celebrated on March 25, making it the date of Jesus' conception and putting his birth nine months later. The liturgical color for Christmas is **white,** commonly used on festival Sundays to reinforce the joy of the festival. White is also the color of the deity.

Epiphany

The feast of ***Epiphany*** (coming from the Greek word for "to manifest" or "to reveal") is one of the oldest Christian feasts. It originally commemorated four different events, each representing a revelation of God to man: 1) the Nativity, where the angels bore witness to the newborn Christ-child; 2) the visit of the Magi, where Jesus was revealed to the Gentiles; 3) the baptism of Jesus, where God the Father declared Jesus to be his Son; and 4) the first miracle at the wedding in Cana, where Jesus' divinity was revealed to his followers. In the Western Christian Church today, the festival of Epiphany primarily focuses on the Magi's visit. In the Eastern Orthodox Church, the primary focus is on the baptism of Jesus. As with other festival Sundays throughout the church year, the color for the Festival of Epiphany is **white.**

The Christian Church Year

Epiphany is also a season of the church year. Depending on the date of Ash Wednesday, the season of Epiphany consists of four to eight Sundays. This season celebrates the many different ways that Jesus is revealed as the Savior of the world. The season is bookended by festivals that typify the revealing of Jesus' divinity: the Baptism of Our Lord (the first Sunday after the Epiphany) and Transfiguration (the last Sunday after the Epiphany). On the other Sundays in the Epiphany season, we see Jesus revealed as the promised Messiah through his miracles, ministry, message, and mission work.

The liturgical color for the other Sundays during the season of Epiphany (with the exception of the Baptism of Our Lord and Transfiguration) is **green**. Green is used both for the Sundays after Epiphany and the Sundays after Pentecost, making it the most commonly used color during the church year. The color green is associated with growth. During the Epiphany season, a season celebrating Jesus' revealing as the Savior of the world, *green* marks the growth of the Church as this Savior is proclaimed to the nations.

Baptism of Our Lord

On the first Sunday after the Epiphany, Anglican and Lutheran churches celebrate the festival of the ***Baptism of Our Lord.*** This festival fits well with the season of Epiphany: a season which focuses on the different ways that Jesus is revealed as the Savior of the world. At Jesus' baptism, he is revealed as a person of the Trinity and as the Anointed One—the Christ, the Messiah (both of these titles mean "the Anointed One"). At Jesus' baptism, God anointed him with the Holy Spirit and with power. He declared this son of Mary to be the Son of God, the one anointed as the Savior of mankind. On the festival of the Baptism of our Lord, we also remember our own baptism, when we were gathered into God's family by water and the Word. As with other festival Sundays throughout the church year, the color for the Baptism of Our Lord is **white** because Jesus was revealed as true God at his baptism.

Transfiguration

On the Roman calendar, the ***Transfiguration of our Lord*** occurs on August 6. The Lutheran reformers, however, moved the observation of Transfiguration to the end of the Epiphany season. During Epiphany, we focus on how Jesus showed himself to be the Son of God and the Savior of the world through word and deed. Transfiguration reveals a glimpse of Jesus in all his divine glory and offers a preview of Easter morning. Therefore, it is particularly appropriate to celebrate Transfiguration on the last Sunday after Epiphany, before the Church descends into the shadowy valley of Lent. As with other festival Sundays throughout the church year, the color for Transfiguration is **white,** again because Jesus was revealed as true God at the Transfiguration.

■ The Christian Church Year

Lent

Ash Wednesday marks the beginning of **Lent,** the Church's 40 day journey of repentance and renewal in preparation for Holy Week. The word Lent comes from an old English word that means "to lengthen" or simply "spring." It is during these days of late winter and early spring that the hours of daylight grow longer. Lent is a 40 day season of repentance, renewal, and preparation for the events of Holy Week and Easter. In the early Christian Church, catechumens (those studying the faith) were instructed during Lent. "Alleluia" is typically omitted from the liturgy during Lent to reflect the somberness of the season.

Ash Wednesday's strong call for preparation and repentance is carried through in the five midweek Lenten services that follow it, but the theme is not repeated during the Sundays in Lent. These Sundays are not counted in the 40 days of the season, and that is why they are called the Sundays **in** Lent and not the Sundays **of** Lent. Rather, these Sundays serve as islands of refreshment during the somber season, and they remind God's people that every Sunday is a "little Easter."[18]

The liturgical color for Lent is ***purple.*** Like black, purple is a penitential color, representing somberness, repentance, and prayer. During Jesus' time, purple dye was very expensive, making purple a color worn mainly by the rich and by royalty. The soldiers at Jesus' trial mocked him by placing him in a purple robe. Purple is used during Lent as a reminder of the solemn and sacrificial nature of the season.

Ash Wednesday

The 40-day season of Lent begins with the observance of **Ash Wednesday,** which can occur as early as February 4 and as late as March 10. In Biblical times, ashes were used to express grief or sorrow for sins committed. Many Christian churches celebrate Ash Wednesday with the imposition of ashes created from burning the palm branches from the previous year's Palm Sunday. Imposition of ashes is not widely practiced in WELS congregations, not because of any specific objection to the practice, but simply because the practice was not retained at the time of the Reformation.

The liturgical color for Ash Wednesday is ***black.*** Black represents the absence of light. It is used only twice during the church year, on Ash Wednesday and Good Friday. On Ash Wednesday we soberly reflect on the cost of our redemption.

---

[18] Jonathan E. Schroeder, *Planning Christian Worship (Supplemental Lectionary) – Year A* (Authorized by the Commission on Worship of the Wisconsin Evangelical Lutheran Synod), 53.

The Christian Church Year

Palm Sunday

For 1700 years, the Christian Church has celebrated **Palm Sunday**—the festival that opens Holy Week—with "Hosannas" and palm branches.[19] The season of Lent begins with an almost equal focus on the sinner and the Savior. But beginning on Palm Sunday and continuing to increase in intensity throughout Holy Week, the focus is on Christ[20]—the Messiah, our Eternal King, who comes in the name of the Lord. As with the rest of the Sundays in Lent, the liturgical color for Palm Sunday is *purple.*

The events of Palm Sunday are rooted in ancient symbolism. The donkey that Jesus rode on would have been viewed as an animal of humility, ridden by a king when he wanted to emphasize that he was coming in peace rather than waging war. Palm branches were used to cover the path of someone thought worthy of the highest honor (see also 2 Kings 9:13). Of the four Gospel writers, only John specifically identifies the branches that were laid in Jesus' path as palm branches. In Jesus' time, the palm branch symbolized hope, life, and victory. These link to Revelation 7:9, where John sees a heavenly multitude of saints standing before the throne of the Lamb and holding palm branches.

Maundy Thursday

The word *Maundy* comes from the Latin word for commandment *(mandatum),* which Jesus talked about when he said to his disciples, "A new command I give you: Love one another," and "Do this in remembrance of me." **Maundy Thursday** is the first of the "three holy days" on the Christian calendar, followed by Good Friday and Easter. As with the rest of Lent, the liturgical color for Maundy Thursday is *purple.*

Maundy Thursday is more than just the remembrance of an historic event. On this day, we celebrate the Sacrament of Holy Communion instituted by Jesus at the Passover celebration. In this Sacrament, Jesus gives us his body and blood as the personal assurance of his love and our forgiveness. Its institution on Passover emphasizes the establishment of the New Covenant and the fulfillment of the law by Jesus the Lamb of God.

---

[19] Schroeder, *Planning Christian Worship,* 67.
[20] Jonathan E. Schroeder, ed., and Daniel M. Deutschlander, *Planning Christian Worship (Supplemental Lectionary)– Year B – Festival Half* (Authorized by the Commission on Worship of the Wisconsin Evangelical Lutheran Synod), 57.

The Christian Church Year

Good Friday

On **Good Friday,** the Church remembers the crucifixion of her Lord. Her remembrance, while solemn, is not a message of gloom, but a service of adoration of the Son of God as he offers up his life as the Lamb of God. Good Friday is part of the larger celebration of the mystery of salvation beginning on Maundy Thursday and culminating in the proclamation of the Easter message, "He is risen!" The liturgical color for Good Friday is **black,** used only on Ash Wednesday and Good Friday.

To impress upon the hearts and minds of believers the terrible consequences of sin and the magnitude of the Savior's sacrifice, the ancient Church held a special service called the Tenebrae on the last days of Holy Week. Tenebrae is a Latin word meaning "shadows" or "darkness." The gradual extinguishing of the candles and darkening of the sanctuary during the service remind us of the events that led to the awful darkness that covered the earth when our Savior hung on the cross. The climax of the service, the announcement of Christ's death, is accompanied by the *strepitus:* a loud noise symbolic of the closing of the tomb. Although Tenebrae is a solemn service, it is not without hope. As the service concludes, one candle—the Christ Candle—is left burning on the center of the altar to remind us of our Lord's abiding presence.

Easter Vigil

A vigil is a service of Scripture readings and prayers in which believers vigilantly and eagerly wait and watch for the celebration of the Savior's deliverance. Old Testament believers waited through the night of Passover for God to deliver them from the Egyptians. Coming together for a vigil helps believers practice waiting patiently for God to reveal his will in his own time.

The **Easter Vigil** is the most well-known and historic of the Church's vigils. Its general structure is one of the most ancient rites of the Christian Church. Church records indicate that it may have been celebrated in Jerusalem as early as the 2nd century. In the early Church, the Vigil was when the catechumens (those receiving instruction) were baptized and received their first Communion.

The Easter Vigil traditionally consists of four parts. The *Service of Light* focuses the entire Vigil on Christ, the light of the world, who overcame the darkness of sin by his resurrection. The *Service of Readings* focuses on the theme of God's saving acts in history. The *Service of Holy Baptism* identifies baptism as one of God's great acts of deliverance and connects baptism with Christ's resurrection. The last part of the Vigil, the *Service of Holy Communion,* is relatively simple in form and style.

The Christian Church Year

Easter

Easter is both a festival Sunday and a season of the church year. "Among the Sundays of the year, Easter Sunday has the place of prominence. On this day, the Church celebrates the resurrection of Christ from death and the restoration of life to those dead in trespasses and sins."[21] The early Church established the celebration of Easter sometime in the 2nd century. Easter is a movable feast—that is, its date changes from year to year. In the Western Church, Easter always falls between March 22 and April 25. It is celebrated on the Sunday following the first full moon after the vernal equinox (March 21).

The Easter season is fifty days long and consists of eight Sundays: from Easter to Pentecost. The season of Easter is the oldest season in the church year, referred to as early as the 3rd century. The Sundays of Easter remind us that Easter is more than just one day on the calendar. Instead, it is a continued celebration of Jesus' resurrection from the dead and victory over Satan. The liturgical color for Easter is ***white,*** reflecting the joy and purity of the risen Christ. Gold is an alternate color for Easter, symbolizing riches, victory, and royalty.

During the Easter season, the first lesson comes from the book of Acts. Acts serves as a bridge for the writings of the New Testament. It tells of the birth and infancy of the Christian church—the 30 years between the events occurring in the Gospels and the writing of the epistles. As we hear of the spread of the Gospel in the early Church, we also consider the Easter joy which should manifest itself in the spread of the Gospel today.

Ascension

The festival of ***Ascension*** is celebrated on the 40th day after Easter—the Thursday between the Sixth and Seventh Sundays of Easter. On Ascension, we celebrate our risen Lord's return to his Father in heaven. There he sits at God's right hand, interceding for us and preparing our eternal home. Because of Jesus' resurrection and completion of his work as marked by his ascension, we too have certainty that we will share in his heavenly glory. The liturgical color for Ascension is ***white,*** reinforcing the joy of Ascension and our sure and certain hope of heaven.

---

[21] Baumler and Moldenhauer, *Manual*, 370.

■ The Christian Church Year

Pentecost

For New Testament believers, **Pentecost** marks the 50th day after Easter and is commemorated as the birthday of the Christian Church. But Pentecost was first celebrated in the Old Testament as the feast of Shavuot, also known as the Festival of Weeks. It occurred seven weeks after Passover (generally during the modern-day months of May or June) and was primarily an agricultural festival. God's Old Testament people celebrated the gathering of the harvest at Pentecost by bringing an offering of firstfruits of their new grain to the Lord. Shavuot was one of three Old Testament festivals which required all Israelite men to make a pilgrimage to the temple at Jerusalem.

The liturgical color for Pentecost is **red.** The color red denotes the power of the Holy Spirit and the tongues of fire which came to rest on the apostles' heads. The word Pentecost comes from the Greek and literally means "five times ten"—the number of days Shavuot was celebrated after Passover in the Old Testament and the number of days Pentecost is celebrated after Easter in the New Testament.

Trinity Sunday

In the Western Church, the first Sunday after Pentecost is designated as *Trinity Sunday.* Trinity Sunday marks the beginning of the non-festival half of the church year. The festival half of the church year (consisting of Advent through Pentecost) focuses on the life of Christ. Beginning with Trinity Sunday and continuing through the Sundays of End Times, the focus shifts to the life of the Christian. Christ and his work of salvation is always our focus throughout the church year, but now the readings emphasize the result of this work through the Word. During the Sundays after Pentecost, we focus on our faith—its creation, growth, and fruit in our lives.[22] As with other festival Sundays throughout the church year, the color for Trinity Sunday is **white.**

Sundays after Pentecost

The first Sunday after Pentecost (Trinity Sunday) begins the non-festival half of the church year. Depending on the date of Easter, this season consists of 19 to 24 Sundays, with the Sundays of End Time counted separately. The **Sundays after Pentecost** focus on Jesus' teachings and the growth of our faith. The color for the Sundays after Pentecost is **green.** Green is the color of growth and new life. Through study of the Word and regular participation in the Sacraments, our faith grows and is strengthened by Christ.

---

[22] Schroeder and Deutschlander, *Planning Christian Worship*, 88.

The Christian Church Year

Along with the Sundays after Epiphany, the Sundays after Pentecost are known as *ordinary time*. When combined, these two seasons make up the majority of the church year. By focusing on Jesus' teachings during these seasons, ordinary time is a time for growth in the life of the Christian. Ordinary time concludes with the last Sunday of the church year: Christ the King Sunday.

End Times

The last four Sundays of the church year are designated as the season of **End Times.** This season, unique to *Christian Worship,* focuses on fulfillment of Christ's promises and encouragement for the Church of the End Times. The Sundays in this season prepare the Church for these latter days by encouraging faithfulness to the Word (Reformation, ***red),*** mindfulness of the judgment (Last Judgment, ***red),*** watchfulness for Christ's coming (Saints Triumphant, ***white),*** and joyfulness in Christ's reign (Christ the King, ***white).***[23] Jesus calls on us to remember his promise: "Behold, I am coming soon!"

---

[23] Schroeder, *Planning Christian Worship,* 160.

The Books of the Bible

The Books of the Bible

The importance of the Bible cannot be overstated. In it, God speaks to us through his divinely inspired words. He tells of the creation of the world and the fall into sin. He tells of his perfect plan to send a Savior to redeem his fallen creation. He tells of the history of his chosen people and further unfolds his plan of salvation. He tells of the birth of this Savior when the time had fully come. He tells of the Savior's perfect life, innocent death, triumphant resurrection, and glorious ascension. And he tells us how to live as we await the Savior's return on the last day.

No special knowledge is needed to read and understand God's message presented in the Bible. Anyone can pick up the book and comprehend what God has done for us. But the Bible's message is richer and more meaningful with added context and background knowledge.

These Biblical notes are intended to provide that context and knowledge. By providing historical and literary background for each Biblical book, we hope to deepen your understanding of the Bible as a whole. In the Bible, sixty-six books paint a complete picture of God's plan of salvation. Understanding how these books fit together makes that painting more alive and vibrant. It also clearly brings out the central focus of the painting: Jesus, the Son of God, the One who saves his people from their sins. May you always keep this focus front and center as you read and study God's inspired Word.

Old Testament Biblical Notes

Genesis

Genesis is a book of beginnings. One of its main focuses is that of relationships: between God and nature, God and man, and man and man. Genesis clearly teaches that there is one true God and emphasizes his sovereignty over his entire creation. Through the accounts in Genesis, we are introduced to the way God initiates and makes covenants with his chosen people, pledging his love and faithfulness to them and calling upon them to pledge the same.

Genesis is the foundation for understanding the rest of the Biblical message. The cycle of sin, judgment, and grace is seen over and over throughout the course of the book. In Genesis, we see the first promise of the Messiah (Genesis 3:15) and one of the oldest and most profound definitions of faith (Genesis 15:6). Although the book was likely written almost 3,500 years ago, its message is still relevant today. Many of the subjects and themes of the first three chapters of Genesis are mirrored in the last three chapters of Revelation.

Exodus

In Hebrew, the first five books of the Old Testament (known as the Pentateuch) are thought of as a single narrative. Although Exodus presents its own themes and message, it should also be understood as a continuation of the history of the Israelites begun in Genesis. In Exodus, we hear primarily of the Israelites' departure from Egypt, the giving of the law at Mount Sinai, and instructions for the construction of the tabernacle and for worship. The central figure in the book is Moses.

Exodus is rich in theology. Throughout the book, God reveals his name, his attributes, his redemption, his law, and how he is to be worshiped. He shows himself to be a God who keeps his promises, especially the promises of deliverance, land, and descendants made to Abraham, Isaac, and Jacob. The themes of sacrifice and redemption resound throughout the book, especially as seen in the first Passover (chapter 12) and the establishment of the covenant (chapter 24).

The Books of the Bible

Leviticus

Leviticus (coming from the Greek for "relating to the Levites") focuses mainly on worship conducted at the tabernacle by the sons of Aaron. Continuing the instructions for building the tabernacle given in Exodus, Leviticus provides regulations for worship in this tabernacle. The book establishes the various types of offerings the Israelites were to bring, describes the duties and requirements of the office of the high priest, and creates the feasts or festivals the Israelites used to order their year.

The main theme of Leviticus is holiness: the holiness of God and the corresponding holiness he demands from his chosen people. Through the strict requirements for sacrifice and the laws governing every aspect of the Israelites' daily lives, God established his sovereignty over his chosen people. All these sacrifices clearly point ahead to the perfect sacrifice that would be offered nearly 1500 years later by Christ, the Messiah.

Numbers

The book of Numbers receives its name from two census lists of Israelite men 20 years of age or older who were able to serve in the army. The first census was taken immediately after the Israelites left Egypt (chapter 1) and the second was taken almost 40 years later as the Israelites were preparing to enter the promised land of Canaan (chapter 26).

The Hebrew title of the book—*Bemidbar*, or "in the desert"—is much more descriptive of its contents. Numbers recounts the story of Israel's journey through the desert from Mount Sinai to the plains of Moab on the border of Canaan. Although its ancient contents tell of the rebellion of Israel against the God who delivered them from slavery, the message of Numbers has lasting significance for the church. God displays his wrath against his disobedient and straying people, but his grace is always renewed and his redemptive purposes will always come to fruition.

Deuteronomy

The book of Deuteronomy, meaning "repetition of the law" or literally "second law," is the fifth book of the Old Testament. The book consists of Moses' farewell addresses delivered to the Israelites before transferring leadership to Joshua. These addresses were intended to prepare the Israelites to enter the promised land of Canaan and emphasize the laws that were especially needed on the eve of conquering the land. "In contrast to the matter-of-fact narratives of Leviticus and Numbers, the book of Deuteronomy comes to us from Moses' heart in a warm, personal, sermonic form of expression."[24]

---

[24] Robert G. Hoerber, ed. *Concordia Self-Study Bible, New International Version* (St. Louis: Concordia Publishing House, 1986), 242.

Central to the book is the covenant relationship of love between the Lord and his people. The focus of Deuteronomy—total commitment to the Lord in worship and obedience to his laws and commands—makes its relevance timeless. In the New Testament, Deuteronomy is quoted or alluded to almost 100 times. The book shows us the heart of God: both his justice through the Law and his mercy through the Gospel.

Joshua

The book of Joshua tells a story of conquest and covenant promises fulfilled in the lives of God's people. After many years of slavery in Egypt and 40 years of wandering in the desert, the Israelites were finally allowed to enter the land promised to their forefathers. Joshua begins where Deuteronomy ends: with the 12 tribes of Israel camped on the east side of the Jordan River. The book "opens with God's command to move forward and pass through the river on dry land."[25] It then tells of a series of military victories that gave the Israelites control of much of the land of Canaan. Although Israel's conquest of the promised land continued after the events recorded in Joshua, the theme of the book is this conquest of Canaan.

In Joshua, a historical figure and the leader of the Israelites, we clearly see a portrayal of God's grace. Earlier in his life, Joshua was simply called Hoshea, meaning "salvation." Moses later changed his name to Joshua, which means "The LORD saves" or "The LORD gives victory." This name is the Hebrew equivalent of the Greek name "Jesus." Joshua is an Old Testament type or foreshadowing of Jesus. He serves as God's chosen servant to bring Moses' work to completion and lead the Israelites into the land of Canaan.

Judges

Judges tells of Israelite history in the promised land from the death of Joshua to the beginning of the monarchy. The book is named for the leaders, or judges, whom God raised up during this time. The time of the judges is best characterized by a recurring phrase in the book: "In those days Israel had no king; everyone did as he saw fit" (Judges 17:6). Judges clearly shows the cycle which would plague the Israelites for much of their time in the promised land: disobedience, foreign oppression, cries of distress, and deliverance.

Throughout the recurring cycle of spiritual failure, God's love and covenant faithfulness clearly shines. Of all the Old Testament books, Judges best contrasts Israel's unfaithfulness with the faithfulness and mercy of God. The judges that God raised up to deliver his people also foreshadow the ultimate deliverance that would come one day through Christ.

---

[25] Hoerber, *Self-Study Bible*, 287.

Ruth

The book of Ruth takes place during the period of the judges, a dark time in Israel's history when "Israel had no king; everyone did as he saw fit" (Judges 17:6). It is one of only two Biblical books named for a woman (the other being the book of Esther). Ruth is a Hebrew short story which focuses primarily on the private lives of one Israelite family. The true faith of Ruth, Naomi, and Boaz is contrasted with the overwhelming unfaithfulness of the Israelites during the time of the judges. A key theme of the narrative is redemption; the Hebrew word in its various forms appears 23 times throughout the short story.

The unknown author of the book focuses on Ruth's unwavering and selfless devotion to desolate Naomi and on Boaz's kindness to these two widows. It may seem surprising that Ruth, the one who reflects God's love so clearly, is a Moabitess. In spite of her heritage, her complete devotion to her mother-in-law and to the one true God mark her as a redeemed daughter of Israel. She is an ancestor of King David and is one of only four women mentioned in Matthew's genealogy of Jesus.

Samuel

1 and 2 Samuel were written as a single literary work. This book was divided into two parts by the translators of the Septuagint (the Greek translation of the Old Testament). It is named for the prophet Samuel, the person God used to establish the monarchy in Israel. Both of Israel's first two kings, Saul and David, were anointed by Samuel. His importance as God's representative is similar to that of Moses. Samuel was instrumental in the continuity of the covenant during the transition from the rule of the judges to the reign of kings. 1 and 2 Samuel chronicle the history of Israel from the birth of Samuel to the end of David's kingship.

Kings

Like 1 and 2 Samuel, 1 and 2 Kings were written as a single literary work, simply called "Kings" in Hebrew tradition. The division of this work into two books was introduced by the translators of the Septuagint (the Greek translation of the Old Testament). The unknown author of 1 and 2 Kings selected and arranged his material in a manner that provides a sequel to the history presented in 1 and 2 Samuel. Throughout this history, the role of the monarchy in light of God's covenant is always emphasized.

In general, 1 and 2 Kings cover the time period from the beginning of Solomon's reign to the Babylonian captivity. Contrary to secular historical methods, attention is not necessarily given to those kings whose reigns have significant political importance. Rather, the kings who receive the most attention in 1 and 2 Kings are those whose reigns reflect one of two opposite attitudes: exceptional adherence to or exceptional deviation from God's covenant.

Chronicles

As with 1 and 2 Samuel and 1 and 2 Kings, 1 and 2 Chronicles were originally written as a single literary work. According to ancient Jewish tradition, Ezra wrote Chronicles, but there is no concrete evidence to support this view. The author of Chronicles used a number of written sources to compile his history, drawing about half his work from Samuel and Kings. There are also frequent references to other books of the kings not included in the Old Testament.

The book was likely written after Judah's return from captivity in Babylon. "[The author] did not invent, but he did select, arrange, and integrate his sources to compose a narrative 'sermon' for postexilic Israel as she struggled to reorient herself as the people of God in a new situation."[26] Several themes throughout the book link this postexilic nation with the Israel of old: the temple in Jerusalem (both Solomon's temple and the rebuilding allowed by Cyrus king of Persia), the continued role of the law and the prophets in Israel's history, and continued hope in the promised Messiah. Much of the book is devoted to the reigns of David and Solomon. There are also extensive genealogies presented.

Ezra

Both Ezra and Nehemiah tell of Judah's return from the Babylonian captivity and the subsequent rebuilding of Jerusalem and the temple. Two main returns are chronicled in Ezra: the first return, led by Zerubbabel (chapters 1-6), with a focus on rebuilding the temple, and the second return, led by Ezra (chapters 7-10), with a focus on rebuilding the spiritual condition of the exiles. Almost 60 years separates these two returns. During this gap, the events of the book of Esther take place.

Ezra contains both first-person and third-person narratives. The writing style of these accounts resemble each other, making it likely that the same author wrote both sections. This author also likely wrote/compiled Chronicles and Nehemiah. Similar literary features are present throughout all four books, such as a proclivity for lists, an emphasis on the Levites and those serving in the temple, and language virtually exclusive to these books.

---

[26] Hoerber, *Self-Study Bible*, 578.

Nehemiah

Both Nehemiah and Ezra tell of Judah's return from the Babylonian captivity and the subsequent rebuilding of Jerusalem and the temple. Nehemiah (meaning "The LORD comforts") focuses on the third return from Babylon and the rebuilding of the wall surrounding Jerusalem. The prophet Malachi also lived at this time. Due to similarities in writing style and emphasis, it is likely that the author of Nehemiah also wrote Chronicles and Ezra.

In the person of Nehemiah (a cupbearer to the king of Persia), a foreshadowing or type of Christ can be seen. "Both [Nehemiah and Christ] give up a high position to identify with the plight of their people; both come with a specific mission; both fulfill it; both show prayerful dependence on God."[27]

Esther

The events of the book of Esther occur c. 460 B.C., between the first and second returns of Judah from the Babylonian captivity. The book records the institution of the annual festival of Purim. This festival celebrates the deliverance of the Jewish people from their enemies during the reign of Xerxes. The author of Esther is unknown, but based on the emphasis given to Purim, he must have been a Jew.

One interesting feature of the book is the lack of any explicit reference to God, worship, prayer, or sacrifice. "However, it appears that the author has deliberately refrained from mentioning God or any religious activity as a literary device to heighten the fact that it is God who controls and directs all the seemingly insignificant coincidences . . . God's sovereign rule is assumed at every point, an assumption made all the more effective by the total absence of reference to him."[28]

Job

The central theme of the book of Job is suffering. From a human perspective, the suffering of the righteous man Job appears arbitrary and undeserved. From a divine perspective, this suffering is used to test, teach, and achieve God's ultimate purposes. Job likely lived during the time of the judges, although the book (whose author is unknown) was written later, anytime from Solomon's reign to the Babylonian exile. The book contains both Hebrew prose (prologue and epilogue) and poetry (main body). Its literary structure and language are among some of the most beautiful in the Old Testament.

---

[27] Hoerber, *Self-Study Bible*, 692.
[28] Hoerber, *Self-Study Bible*, 718.

The message proclaimed to Job is extremely relevant for Christians today. In the book, we are given an intimate glimpse into conversations between God and Satan. We also hear God speak to Job and instruct him in his ways. One of the most well-loved hymns finds its inspiration in Job: "I know that my Redeemer lives, and that in the end he will stand upon the earth . . . I myself will see him with my own eyes . . . how my heart yearns within me!" (Job 19:25-27)

Psalms

Psalms is the hymnal of the Old Testament. It was likely compiled into its final form in the 3rd century B.C. It served as a book of prayer and praise in the post-exilic temple and in the Jewish synagogues. Individual psalms were likely used in worship during the reigns of David and Solomon. Its name comes from a Greek word meaning a song sung to the music of a harp.

Psalms is divided into five books (Psalms 1-41, 42-72, 73-89, 90-106, and 107-150). Each book concludes with a doxology. In addition, Psalms 1-2 serve as an introduction for the entire book and Psalms 146-150 as a conclusion. Two-thirds of the psalms have an attributed author. Psalms of Moses, David, Solomon, and Asaph are included in the book. The psalms can be divided into categories in any number of ways. Luther placed the psalms into five categories: Messianic, teaching/doctrine, comfort, prayer/petition, and thanksgiving/praise. Psalms is quoted numerous times in the New Testament, with Jesus often using poetry from Psalms to refer to himself.

Proverbs

Proverbs is one of five Old Testament books classified as "wisdom literature" (along with Job, Psalms, Ecclesiastes, and Song of Songs). Wisdom literature is a genre of writing that focuses on existential questions about God, humanity, and the nature of evil and suffering. Proverbs is one of the more optimistic works of wisdom literature. It provides advice on how to behave and live in order to have a prosperous and happy life. However, it is crucial to interpret the proverbs as general statements about the nature of life and not as specific promises or prophecies.

Many of the proverbs were written by Solomon, but there are other authors mentioned as well. Chapter 30 is attributed to Agur son of Jakeh and chapter 31 to King Lemuel. Neither of these men are mentioned elsewhere in Scripture. As referenced in Proverbs 25:1, Hezekiah's men copied and compiled some of the proverbs. It is possible, however, that the compilation of Proverbs as it exists today was not completed until after Hezekiah's reign.

Ecclesiastes

Ecclesiastes receives its name from the Greek word for "Teacher" (*ekklesiastes*), the one whose words make up the book. The author of the book does not identify himself beyond calling himself "son of David" (1:1), where the Hebrew word for "son" can also refer more generally to a descendent. The book is commonly attributed to Solomon, written during the later stages of his life, but this authorship is not certain.

"Ecclesiastes emphasizes that life from the human perspective — without the grace of God — is empty and futile."[29] Without God, nothing can satisfy human wants and desires. In contrast, with God, man can enjoy life as a gift and live it to the full within God's commands and will.

Song of Songs

Song of Songs is also known as "Solomon's Song of Songs" or simply "Song of Solomon," indicating a book that was written about, by, or for Solomon. It is possible that Solomon was the author, but like Ecclesiastes his authorship is not certain. The structure of the book and its unity of literary style and tone argue for a single author rather than a compiled work. Its title means the greatest of songs, much like "God of gods" or "King of kings."

A surface glance at Song of Songs shows a picture of love and desire between a shepherd and his beloved. "In Lutheran circles, however, the allegorical interpretation is more general, illustrating . . . Israel as the bride of God and . . . the relationship between the Christian church and Christ. The Song then symbolizes God's grace in his love for his covenant people Israel and in Jesus' love for his bride, the Christian church."[30]

Isaiah

Isaiah (meaning "the LORD saves") was a contemporary of Amos, Hosea, and Micah. He began his ministry in 740 B.C. during the period of Israel's decline and the expansion of the Assyrian empire. Isaiah's prophecies look ahead to the future of the nation of Israel and span nearly 200 years of Old Testament history. In addition, he prophesies about the coming Messiah and "the day of the LORD." Isaiah is often thought of as the greatest of the writing prophets. The beauty of his poetry is unsurpassed in the Old Testament.

---

[29] Hoerber, *Self-Study Bible*, 992.
[30] Hoerber, *Self-Study Bible*, 1005.

The structure of Isaiah is like a miniature Bible. The first 39 chapters (compare with 39 books in the Old Testament) depict judgment and condemnation on an immoral and idolatrous people. The last 27 chapters (compare with 27 books in the New Testament) declare a message of comfort and hope. God is "the Holy One of Israel" who must punish his rebellious people but will afterward redeem them. Isaiah prophesies more clearly and in more ways about the coming Messiah than any other prophet. Some of the best-known and most well-loved prophecies foretelling the birth of Jesus come from the book of Isaiah, especially 7:14, 9:2-7, and 11:1-9.

Jeremiah

Jeremiah prophesied to the southern nation of Judah during the last years of independence before the Babylonian captivity. He was a contemporary of Habakkuk and possibly Obadiah and prophesied in the time period immediately preceding Ezekiel. More is known about Jeremiah's personal life than any other Old Testament prophet. He was a priest from the town of Anathoth (near Jerusalem). At the Lord's command, he neither married nor had children. Jeremiah is often referred to as the "weeping prophet" because his message is so often characterized by anguish of spirit.

Jeremiah foretold the Babylonian captivity and the destruction of the kingdom of Judah. In his book, he shows a particular contempt for false prophets who were foretelling "life as usual" for Judah. "Judgment is one of the all-pervasive themes in Jeremiah's writings, though he was careful to point out that repentance, if sincere, would avert the inevitable."[31] He calls for the people of Judah to repent and promises the restoration of a remnant who would return to the land promised to Abraham.

Lamentations

Lamentations is commonly ascribed to the prophet Jeremiah. The author of the book does not identify himself, but based on laments in Jeremiah and a similar vocabulary and style between the two books, Jeremiah is a likely author. Lamentations vividly portrays the destruction of Jerusalem and its temple, and the exile of its people at the hands of the Babylonians. Laments are found in almost all Old Testament prophetic books, but Lamentations is the only book consisting solely of laments.

---

[31] Hoerber, *Self-Study Bible*, 1119.

Lamentations is a book of poetry and is divided into five laments. The middle lament contains 66 verses and the other four contain 22. The first four laments are acrostic poems, using the letters of the Hebrew alphabet to begin each poetry verse. The high point of the book occurs in the middle lament, where the author focuses on the goodness of God. In spite of the destruction and judgment surrounding his chosen people, "[the LORD's] compassions never fail, they are new every morning." (Lamentations 2:22, 23)

Ezekiel

Ezekiel (meaning "God strengthens") was one of the Jews exiled to Babylon by Nebuchadnezzar in 597 B.C. While in Babylon, Ezekiel was called to be a prophet of God. Despite living under a foreign government, Ezekiel had a relatively free existence. He was married and lived in a house of his own. His writings span approximately 20 years and encompass some of the darkest days in Israel's history: the exile to Babylon, the fall of Jerusalem, and the destruction of the temple.

In some ways, Ezekiel's message is similar to that of other Old Testament prophets with its focus on Israel's idolatry and rebellion against the Lord. Unique to Ezekiel, however, is his focus on Israel as a holy nation—one which would be restored to Jerusalem, the holy city with God's holy temple. Because of Israel's rampant idolatry, God allowed his people to be carried off to captivity and their temple and city destroyed. Yet despite this destruction, a remnant would eventually return and rebuild the temple and the city of Jerusalem because of God's faithfulness to his covenant. In the second half of the book, Ezekiel proclaims this message of consolation and hope to a people living in exile.

Daniel

The book of Daniel (meaning "God is my judge") was written during the Babylonian captivity. Daniel is the last of five books classified as the major prophets. Throughout the book, the sovereignty of God is emphasized. God is described as the one who rules over the kingdoms of men, and he always triumphs in Daniel's visions.

The second half of Daniel is apocalyptic in nature: writing that includes dreams or visions, unusual symbolic imagery, number symbolism, and a focus on events of the end times. This style of writing is also found primarily in the book of Revelation.

The Books of the Bible

Hosea

Hosea (meaning "salvation") prophesied to the northern kingdom of Israel during the final days before its defeat at the hands of the Assyrians. A contemporary of Amos, Hosea prophesied for at least 38 years. Virtually nothing is known about him other than the information presented in this book.

In the first three chapters of Hosea, God provides an object lesson displaying his love for his people Israel despite their spiritual adultery and unfaithfulness. Hosea is instructed to take Gomer, an adulterous woman, as his wife. He was ordered to keep loving her in spite of her unfaithfulness. Gomer's redemption from slavery by Hosea clearly portrays God's love for his covenant people and his willingness to forgive. The second part of the book (chapters 4-14) call Israel to repentance for their worship of Canaanite idols.

Joel

Joel (meaning "The LORD is God") does not specify the time at which he lived and preached. There are no events referenced in Joel which can be dated using non-Biblical sources. Some Bible scholars place the book in the 9th century B.C., making Joel a contemporary of Hosea and Amos. Others date it after the Babylonian captivity and after the writings of Haggai and Zechariah. "In either case, its message is not significantly affected by its dating."[32]

A theme throughout Joel is the coming "day of the LORD." Joel uses a coming plague of locusts on Judah (which is understood to be a real event) to draw parallels to God's judgment on the day of the LORD. Unlike false prophets of his time, Joel does not convey the message that this day will be a day of destruction only for nations other than Israel and Judah. Instead, he proclaims God's judgment on his chosen people as well as on other nations. Joel calls Judah to repent and promises blessings after judgment.

Amos

Amos (meaning "burden" or "burden bearer") was a shepherd from Tekoa, a small town near Bethlehem and Jerusalem in the nation of Judah. He was called to proclaim God's judgment on the northern kingdom of Israel. His ministry likely took place mainly in 760–750 B.C. during the reign of Jeroboam II in Israel and Uzziah in Judah. This was a time of great prosperity and idolatry for both kingdoms. Amos is a contemporary of Isaiah, Hosea, Jonah, and possibly Joel.

---

[32] Hoerber, *Self-Study Bible*, 1342.

In his prophecies, Amos proclaims God's justice and righteousness. He rebukes Israel for the meaninglessness of their worship and their idolatrous practices. His message shows that God is not pleased with worship which is outwardly correct but inwardly spiritually empty. Amos also calls for social justice, "condemning all who make themselves powerful or rich at the expense of others."[33] Despite his harsh words, he still proclaims God's love and hope for redemption if Israel repents (Amos 5:15).

Obadiah

Obadiah (meaning "servant of the LORD" or "worshiper of the LORD") is the shortest book in the Old Testament. Depending on the historical event linked to verses 11-14, Obadiah can be dated to one of two time periods: 853-841 B.C., making him a contemporary of Elisha, or 605-586 B.C., making him a contemporary of Jeremiah. The second dating seems more likely, but Biblical scholars are widely divided.

Obadiah prophesies mainly against the nation of Edom, a people descended from Esau. Throughout the history of God's chosen people, Israel and Edom have had a contentious and sometimes openly hostile relationship. Obadiah reassures Israel that Edom "will be destroyed, but Mount Zion and Israel will be delivered, and God's kingdom will triumph."[34] The brief prophecy closes with a renewal of the promise that Israel will occupy the land of Canaan.

Jonah

Jonah (meaning "dove") was from the tribe of Zebulun. He lived at the time of Jeroboam II in Israel and was a contemporary of Isaiah, Hosea, Amos, and possibly Joel. Jonah was called to preach God's judgment to the city of Nineveh, the capital city of the Assyrian empire. This calling to preach to a Gentile nation clearly shows that God's grace is for all people.

Unlike most other Old Testament books of prophecy, Jonah is a narrative account rather than individual words of prophecy. The extraordinary events of the book (namely the great fish swallowing Jonah) has led to questions as to whether the book portrays actual historical events. There is nothing in the book to indicate that these events did not occur, and so we read them as real events in the life of Jonah. Jesus references the book and compares Jonah's time in the great fish to his time in the tomb (Matthew 12:39-41).

---

[33] Hoerber, *Self-Study Bible*, 1351.
[34] Hoerber, *Self-Study Bible*, 1365.

Micah

Micah (meaning "Who is like the LORD?") was from the town of Moresheth in southern Judah. He prophesied to the southern kingdom of Judah sometime between 750 and 686 B.C. and was a contemporary of Isaiah and Hosea. Micah predicted the fall of Samaria—the capital of Israel—and the ruin which would come upon Judah at the hands of the Babylonians.

Although his message is one of judgment, it is not without hope. In the end, Micah prophesies that gloom will come to triumph and God's people will once again rise over their enemies and live in the light. The book of Micah contains one of the clearest and most specific Messianic prophecies, revealing that the Savior would be born in Bethlehem (Micah 5:2).

Nahum

The only thing known about the prophet Nahum (meaning "comfort") is his hometown of Elkosh, and even its location is uncertain. Nahum prophesied between 663 and 612 B.C., making him a contemporary of Zephaniah and overlapping with the beginning of Jeremiah's ministry. His book contains various oracles against the city of Nineveh, the capital city of the Assyrian empire. The book ends with the predicted destruction of the city.

Since Nahum's prophecy predicted the destruction of one of Israel's great enemies, it would have been a comfort to God's people. Before proclaiming judgment on Nineveh, Nahum details the nature of the LORD, the one who will judge the Assyrians. The LORD's divine attributes of patience, graciousness, and justice are emphasized in the opening chapter of Nahum.

Habakkuk

Habakkuk (probably meaning "one who embraces") lived in Judah sometime around 605 B.C., making him a contemporary of Jeremiah and possibly of Zephaniah. He predicted the Babylonian captivity and the destruction of Jerusalem to the people of Judah. The book, however, does not contain any prophecies addressed directly to Judah. Rather, it is a dialogue between Habakkuk and God—not a private conversation, but a representation of those in Judah who still obeyed God's commands and were struggling to comprehend his ways and his judgment.

Habakkuk begins by questioning God's allowance of evil in Judah. When he is told that this evil will indeed be punished by the Babylonians, he then questions how God can allow a more evil people to execute judgment on Judah. After receiving God's assurance that Babylon will also be punished in turn, Habakkuk closes his book with a beautiful confession of faith in the form of a prayer.

The Books of the Bible

Zephaniah

Zephaniah (meaning "The Lord hides" or "The Lord has hidden") prophesied to the southern kingdom of Judah during the reign of King Josiah. He is a contemporary of Jeremiah, Nahum, and possibly Habakkuk. The book opens with the ancestry of Zephaniah, a fourth-generation descendant of King Hezekiah of Judah. This ancestry indicates that Zephaniah moved in much different social circles than many of the other prophets. His writings show familiarity with the royal courts and political issues of his day.

Like Joel, Zephaniah prophesies about the coming "day of the Lord." Like many of the other prophets, he proclaims destruction and judgment on Judah as punishment for their spiritual unfaithfulness and wickedness. But again like many of the other prophets, his message is not without hope. The book ends with an assurance of God's healing for Judah and a promise to gather the remnant together and bring them home.

Haggai

Haggai (probably meaning "festal" or "festive") wrote during a four-month period in 520 B.C., during the reign of King Darius of Persia. Along with Zechariah, Haggai prophesied during the post-exilic period and encouraged the people of Judah to rebuild the temple in Jerusalem. He also speaks of the coming Messiah, the one who would fill the temple with glory (Haggai 2:9).

After Obadiah, Haggai is the shortest book in the Old Testament. His teachings, however, are no less significant than the other minor prophets. "Haggai clearly shows the consequences of disobedience and obedience. When the people give priority to God and his house, they are blessed rather than cursed. Obedience brings the encouragement and strength of the Spirit of God."[35]

Zechariah

Zechariah (meaning "The Lord remembers" or "The Lord has remembered") was born in Babylon during Judah's time in captivity. He returned to Judah in 538 B.C., making him a contemporary of Ezra, Nehemiah, and Haggai. In addition to being a prophet, Zechariah was also a priest. His message is similar to Haggai's: encouragement to a post-exilic nation to rebuild the temple.

---

[35] Hoerber, *Self-Study Bible*, 1407.

Zechariah contains a number of significant Messianic prophecies. "The prophet foretells the coming of Jesus in lowliness as a 'servant, the Branch' (3:8), who is rejected and sold for 30 pieces of silver (11:12-13), crucified (struck by the sword, 13:7) and pierced (12:10). He is the King-Priest (6:13), the smitten Shepherd (13:7) and the coming Judge and righteous King (14)."[36] The Old Testament lesson for Palm Sunday is from Zechariah 9:9-10 where Jesus' triumphant entry into Jerusalem is anticipated.

Malachi

Malachi (meaning "my messenger") was most likely the last prophet of the Old Testament era and possibly a contemporary of Nehemiah. During the time of Nehemiah's work, the Jews had returned from exile and had rebuilt the temple and the walls of Jerusalem. Since this time, they had once again fallen into sin as detailed in Nehemiah 13:7-31. Malachi specifically condemns several of these sins, including the priests dishonoring God in their sacrifices and not faithfully teaching the law, and the people divorcing and marrying foreign women.

A strong theme in Malachi is the coming of the Lord. He prophesies regarding the coming of the Lord's messenger before the coming of the "day of the LORD." Like many of the other Old Testament prophets, Malachi's prophecies can be viewed in layers: having both an immediate and a far-reaching fulfillment. John the Baptist will serve as the Lord's messenger in the near future. Malachi's prophecies will be fulfilled in full when the Lord comes again on the Last Day.

---

[36] Hoerber, *Self-Study Bible*, 1411.

New Testament Biblical Notes

Matthew

The books of Matthew, Mark, and Luke are classified as the Synoptic Gospels (meaning "seeing together"). They are very similar in language, material, and order of events. The author of the first Gospel is Matthew the apostle, a tax collector who answered Jesus' call to follow him. He is also known as Levi in Mark and Luke's gospels.

Matthew was likely written to Greek-speaking Jews. He emphasizes Jesus as the fulfiller of Old Testament prophecy. The genealogy at the beginning of his book traces Jesus' ancestry back to Abraham, thus establishing Jesus as a legitimate heir of David. Although Matthew was likely writing to Jewish readers, he also emphasizes the universality of God's grace. This can be seen in the inclusion of four women in his genealogy of Jesus, the recounting of the visit by the Magi (Gentiles), and the extending of the Great Commission to all nations.

Mark

The author of the second Gospel was universally acknowledged by the early Church as John Mark, a companion of Paul and Barnabas on their first missionary journey. The early church fathers viewed Mark's Gospel as inspired by the apostle Peter's first-hand accounts of Jesus and his ministry. "The conclusion . . . is that the Gospel of Mark largely consists of the preaching of Peter arranged and shaped by John Mark."[37]

Mark was likely written to Gentile Christians. His book focuses mainly on what Jesus did rather than what he said, although there is also an emphasis on Jesus as a teacher or rabbi. A key phrase in Mark is "immediately" or "at once." Both these English translations come from the same Greek word which is used 47 times throughout the book. Mark is the shortest of the four Gospels.

Luke

The author of this third Gospel does not name himself in the book, but the evidence almost certainly points to the evangelist Luke. Luke was a physician and probably a Gentile. He was a companion of Paul on several of his missionary journeys and also wrote the book of Acts. The books of Luke and Acts were written to Theophilus, possibly the one responsible for copying and distributing the letters.

---

[37] Hoerber, *Self-Study Bible*, 1498.

The focus of the Gospel of Luke is on Jesus as the Messiah and on his mission of salvation. Some of the accounts in Luke also appear in one or more of the other Gospels. However, Luke also presents a number of accounts that are unique to his Gospel. These include the birth of Jesus and Jesus' ministry in Judea and Perea (a region on the east side of the Jordan River).

John

The Gospel of John was written by the apostle John, the "disciple whom Jesus loved." He likely wrote to Christians who were already familiar with the events recounted in Matthew, Mark, and Luke. Therefore, John omits many of these events—in particular, a listing of the twelve apostles and the institution of Holy Communion. John's purpose in writing his Gospel is clear: "these are written that you may believe that Jesus is the Christ, the Son of God, and that by believing you may have life in his name" (John 20:31).

Unique to the Gospel of John is the omission of all parables of Jesus. Instead, John includes seven "I am" statements of Jesus: the bread of life; the light of the world; the gate; the good shepherd; the resurrection and the life; the way, the truth, and the life; and the vine. A key concept in John's Gospel is that of eyewitness testimony of the events in the book.

Acts

On most Sundays during the church year, the first lesson is a reading from the Old Testament. During the six Sundays in the Easter season, this lesson comes instead from the New Testament book of Acts. Acts serves as a bridge for the writings of the New Testament. It tells of the birth and infancy of the Christian church—the 30 years between the events occurring in the Gospels and the writing of the epistles. Luke records the spreading of the gospel from Jerusalem to Rome, the capital and political center of the Roman Empire.

In Acts, we see the apostles with markedly different character than that displayed in the Gospels. These are no longer the same timid disciples who often showed a lack of understanding of Jesus' teachings and who cowed behind locked doors out of fear of the Jewish leaders. Even in the face of persecution, the apostles boldly proclaimed the good news of Jesus' suffering, death, and resurrection. Through the events and preaching chronicled in Acts, the apostles clearly display the power and joy that the risen Christ creates and sustains in the lives of his followers.

The Books of the Bible

Romans

This letter was written by Paul to the church in Rome, likely during the time of his third missionary journey (A.D. 53–57). It was written after 1 and 2 Corinthians and was probably written from the city of Corinth. Paul wrote to the church at Rome, a church that he had not yet visited. The Roman church consisted primarily of Gentile Christians. However, based on the content of Romans (in particular, no difference between Jew and Gentile), there must have been a number of Jewish Christians in the church as well.

Romans focuses squarely on God's most basic plan of salvation for all mankind. Paul focuses on a "righteousness from God" that is revealed in the gospel. "None of Paul's other letters states so profoundly the content of the gospel and its implications."[38] Paul writes very systematically in Romans, presenting his thoughts and teachings more in the form of a theological essay than that of a letter.

1 Corinthians

This letter was written by Paul in approximately A.D. 55 to the believers in Corinth, Greece. Corinth was one of the dominant commercial centers of its time and was located on a major trade route. It was a city famous for both its religious tradition and its extreme immorality. This immorality also plagued the church in Corinth, prompting Paul to write his first letter to the Corinthians. History shows that despite these early struggles, the congregation in Corinth survived and even prospered.

"This letter is timely for the church today, both to instruct and to inspire. Many of the questions and problems that confronted the church at Corinth are still very much with us—problems like immaturity, divisions, jealousy and envy, marital difficulties, sexual immorality, and misuse of spiritual gifts. Yet in spite of this concentration on problems, the book contains some of the most famous and beloved chapters in the entire Bible—for example, chapter 13 (on love) and chapter 15 (on the resurrection)."[39]

---

[38] Hoerber, *Self-Study Bible*, 1715.
[39] Hoerber, *Self-Study Bible*, 1746.

2 Corinthians

2 Corinthians was also written by Paul in approximately A.D. 55 to the believers in Corinth, Greece. 1 Corinthians was likely written in the spring and 2 Corinthians later in the year. The church in Corinth was plagued by false teachers challenging Paul's integrity and authority. Because of a change in his itinerary (visiting Corinth only once instead of twice as initially planned), these false teachers were attacking his reputation and claiming that his teachings were not to be trusted. They also opposed his status as an apostle.

In the book, Paul explains both the reason for the change in his itinerary and his ministry as a whole. He then encourages the Corinthians to prepare for his arrival by completing a collection they had begun the previous year. Finally, Paul defends his status as an apostle and the authority of his teachings. Partially because of this defense, 2 Corinthians contains more personal and autobiographical information than Paul's other letters.

Galatians

This letter was written by Paul to the churches in the Roman province of Galatia. These churches (located in Antioch, Iconium, Lystra, and Derbe) were founded by Paul on his first missionary journey. False teachers had come to these young churches and were preaching a different message than what Paul had taught. These false teachers, known as Judaizers, insisted that faith in the gospel was not sufficient for salvation. Observance of the Old Testament ceremonial law was also necessary, including circumcision. In contrast to these false teachings, Paul emphasizes Christian freedom—freedom from the law through the grace of God.

In Galatians, Paul clearly teaches the basic truths of justification and sanctification. It is by grace alone through faith alone in Jesus Christ alone that we are justified. And it is by this faith alone that we are to live out our new lives in the freedom of the Spirit. This clear teaching of justification by faith alone was a major factor in the Reformation. Galatians is sometimes known as "Luther's book" because Martin Luther heavily used its contents in his writings and arguments against the false teachers and theology of his day.

Ephesians

This letter was written by Paul to believers in the city of Ephesus. At the time, Ephesus was located at an intersection of major trade routes and was an important commercial center of the Roman Empire. As Luke records in Acts, Paul preached and taught for over two years in Ephesus. Ephesians was written while Paul was imprisoned for preaching the gospel, likely in A.D. 60 while he was under house arrest in Rome. Colossians and Philemon were probably written at the same time.

Many of Paul's other letters were written to specifically address some false teaching infiltrating the church. Ephesians does not deal with any such error. "Instead, Paul strives to expand the theological horizons of his readers. He writes so that they might better understand God's eternal purpose and grace and come to appreciate the high goals God has for the church."[40] In a world of confusion, where things do not always make sense, believers look forward to the time when everything will be brought into meaningful relationship under the headship of Christ.

Philippians

Philippians was written to the church in Philippi, a Roman colony whose residents were also citizens of the city of Rome. Paul connects with this theme of citizenship in the letter when he discusses citizenship in heaven (3:20-21). Because the Jewish population of Philippi was relatively small, the city did not have its own synagogue. In addition, the book of Philippians contains no Old Testament quotations, likely demonstrating that Paul is writing to a Gentile audience.

Philippians was written while Paul was under house arrest, probably in A.D. 61 in Rome. During this time, he lived in his own rented house and was able to preach to his visitors. Paul's primary purpose in writing was to thank the Philippians for their generosity upon learning of his imprisonment. He also reports on his own circumstances and encourages the church to stand firm under persecution. One of the letter's primary themes is being joyful—the word "joy" in its various forms occurs 16 times in Philippians. This message is all the more remarkable when considered in light of Paul's imprisonment.

---

[40] Hoerber, *Self-Study Bible*, 1802.

Colossians

This letter was written by Paul to the church in Colosse, a market town located in Asia Minor (present-day Turkey). It likely dates to A.D. 60, during Paul's first imprisonment in Rome. Ephesians and Philemon were also written at this same time while Paul was under house arrest.

In Colossians, Paul wrote in opposition to false teachers who were attacking the young church. This false teaching proclaimed that salvation did not come through Christ alone. To refute this heresy, Paul heavily emphasizes the sufficiency of Christ and the completeness of the salvation he has won for his Church. Though Colossians is one of Paul's shorter letters, it is especially rich with descriptions of Christ, his work, and the blessings he extends to us through holy baptism.

1 Thessalonians

1 Thessalonians was written by Paul to the church in Thessalonica, a Greek port city on the Thermaic Gulf of the Aegean Sea. As chronicled in Acts 17:1-9, Paul visited the Thessalonican church on his second missionary journey but was forced to flee in the middle of the night. The makeup of the church in Thessalonica is not certain, but it was likely primarily Gentile in nature.

Because of Paul's abrupt departure and the persecution that the church was undergoing, new believers were left with little support outside the church. Paul's main purpose in writing 1 Thessalonians was to encourage these new believers in their struggles and give them direction in godly living. Paul also references the second coming of Christ in every chapter of the book, assuring the Thessalonian church that their suffering will be rewarded and perfected on the Last Day.

2 Thessalonians

2 Thessalonians is Paul's second letter to the church in Thessalonica. It was written shortly after 1 Thessalonians, possibly six months later. The church's situation does not appear to have changed much and persecution was still ongoing.

Paul writes for much the same reason as in 1 Thessalonians: to give encouragement and direction in godly living. He also strives to correct several misinterpretations concerning the second coming of Christ as discussed in his first letter. Some of the Thessalonians were concerned that they were to be "blameless" at Jesus' second coming based on their own merits. Paul assures them that this blamelessness is based on God's grace through faith and not on their own works. As with 1 Thessalonians, Paul focuses significantly on the second coming of Christ in this letter.

1 Timothy

1 Timothy was written by Paul to his servant and colleague Timothy. Timothy was a Gentile Christian—his father was Greek and his mother was Jewish. Paul calls him "my true son in the faith," indicating that Timothy may have been one of Paul's converts. Timothy traveled with Paul on several of his missionary journeys and spent time in Ephesus, Macedonia, Corinth, and Asia Minor.

Paul and Timothy amicably parted ways during Paul's fourth missionary journey. Paul went on to Macedonia and instructed Timothy to stay in Ephesus. Paul originally planned to return to Ephesus and continue instructing the church there. When Paul realized that this journey might be delayed, he wrote 1 Timothy to instruct and encourage Timothy in dealing with the Ephesian church. 1 Timothy, 2 Timothy, and Titus are known as the Pastoral Epistles (or letters) because their primary purpose is to instruct Timothy and Titus in the pastoral care of churches.

2 Timothy

2 Timothy was also written by Paul to Timothy, a previous traveling companion of Paul and a current leader of the church at Ephesus. 2 Timothy was written towards the end of Paul's life in A.D. 66-67 after his fourth missionary journey. Paul was again imprisoned for preaching the gospel, this time under Emperor Nero. Unlike his previous imprisonment when he lived in a rented house, Paul was now literally in chains for the gospel. Paul knew that the time had nearly come for his departure. He had fought the good fight, finished the race, and kept the faith (2 Timothy 4:7).

In 2 Timothy, Paul writes to request Timothy's comfort and companionship. Timothy had been caring for the congregation at Ephesus, but Paul sent Tychicus as a replacement so that Timothy, his son in the faith, could travel to him. It is not known whether Timothy ever reached Paul in prison. This is Paul's last known letter, written with special emphasis on faithfully teaching the Word in opposition to false teachers and rising persecution.

Titus

This letter was written by Paul to Titus, a Gentile Christian who was one of Paul's converts. Titus is not mentioned specifically in Acts as being a companion on any of Paul's missionary journeys, but he likely worked with Paul in Ephesus during Paul's third missionary journey. He was then sent to assist the church in Corinth as mentioned in 2 Corinthians. Titus also worked with Paul in Crete and remained there as Paul's representative after Paul's departure.

Paul wrote to Titus to encourage him in his ministry and offer assistance and guidance on problems plaguing the church. This advice, dealing with church elders, false teachers, and faith and conduct in general, is still timely for the church today.

Philemon

This letter was written by Paul to Philemon, a believer and a member of the church in Colosse. It was likely written at the same time as Colossians and sent with the same couriers. Philemon was a slave owner. One of his slaves, Onesimus, ran away—an act punishable by death under Roman law. Through Onesimus' flight, he met Paul and became a Christian. Paul sent Onesimus back to Philemon and asked for mercy on Onesimus' behalf.

Although the direct circumstances of the letter are not replicated in our world today, the message of the letter should still resound. "We are, like Onesimus, guilty of sin. Jesus' ministry on earth and mediation before his Father parallel Paul's advocacy before Philemon. We, like Onesimus, are condemned by law, but saved by God's grace."[41]

Hebrews

This letter was addressed primarily to Jewish Christians, possibly living in Rome, who were familiar with the Old Testament. The writer of the letter does not identify himself. The book was originally called "The Epistle of Paul to the Hebrews" (from approximately A.D. 400 to 1600). However, due mainly to differing emphases and writing styles, since the Reformation it has been widely acknowledged that Paul could not have been the author. Possible authors include Barnabas, one of Paul's companions on his missionary journeys, and Apollos, a Jewish Christian in Corinth with a "thorough knowledge of the Scriptures" (Acts 18:24). Its date is also uncertain, although it must have been written before the destruction of the temple in A.D. 70.

Because the recipients of the letter to the Hebrews were being tempted to revert to Judaism, the author provides a detailed discussion of the person and work of Jesus Christ as Prophet, Priest, and King. Over 20 titles are used to describe Jesus' attributes and accomplishments. Hebrews also focuses on the absolute supremacy and sufficiency of Christ. Jesus offered himself as the one final sacrifice for sin, a sacrifice far superior to the animal sacrifices required by Old Testament law. Through Jesus our great High Priest, we have a new covenant with God. "Hebrews could be called 'the book of better things' since the Greek words for 'better' and 'superior' appear 15 times in the letter."[42]

---

[41] Hoerber, *Self-Study Bible*, 1870.
[42] Hoerber, *Self-Study Bible*, 1874.

James

The author of this letter simply identifies himself as "James." Of the four men in the New Testament with this name, the most likely author is James the half-brother of Jesus. He is referenced a number of times throughout the New Testament as a leader and "pillar" of the church. In Acts 15, he is mentioned as being a member of the council of Jerusalem.

The recipients of the letter were likely Jewish Christians—originally from the church in Jerusalem and then scattered after the death of Stephen and the subsequent persecution that followed. "As leader of the Jerusalem church, James wrote as pastor to instruct and encourage his dispersed people in the face of their difficulties."[43] James emphasizes how Christian faith should show itself in daily living.

1 Peter

The apostle Peter identifies himself as the author of this letter. Some question Peter's authorship due to the fact that the Greek used in the letter is good literary Greek, likely beyond the fisherman Peter's ability. This can be explained by 1 Peter 5:12, where Peter says he wrote "with the help of Silas." Silas likely served as a secretary for the writing of 1 Peter and composed Peter's thoughts into better written Greek than Peter himself would have used.

1 Peter was written to "strangers in the world, scattered throughout Pontus, Galatia, Cappadocia, Asia, and Bithynia" (1 Peter 1:1). The recipients likely included both Jewish and Gentile Christians. This letter touches on a number of themes, most of which are primarily connected to the life and duties of a Christian. "It has been characterized as a letter of separation, of suffering and persecution, of suffering and glory, of hope, of pilgrimage, of courage, and as a letter dealing with the true grace of God."[44]

2 Peter

As with 1 Peter, the apostle Peter identifies himself as the author of this letter. 2 Peter is somewhat different in style than 1 Peter, leading some to question a common author of the two books. This can be explained by noting that Silas likely served as a secretary for the writing of 1 Peter (1 Peter 5:12), but Silas is not referenced in connection with 2 Peter. There are also similarities between 2 Peter and Jude that suggest one author borrowed from the other.

---

[43] Hoerber, *Self-Study Bible*, 1897.
[44] Hoerber, *Self-Study Bible*, 1904.

In this letter, Peter focuses on equipping his readers to deal with false teachers within the church. He calls upon his own eyewitness testimony of events in Jesus' life to establish his authority as a true preacher of the Word. He then assures his readers that in the last days, these false teachers will indeed come, but God will set all things right on the Last Day. The letter closes with an encouragement to "be on your guard" and "grow in the grace and knowledge of our Lord and Savior Jesus Christ" (2 Peter 5:17,18).

1 John

This letter was written by the apostle John, the "disciple whom Jesus loved." John does not specifically identify himself as the author in the letter, but the style, content, and phrasing of this letter are all very similar to the Gospel of John. Its date of writing is uncertain, but John's use of "children" for his readers suggests that he wrote this letter later in his life, likely between A.D. 85 and 95 — after the writing of his Gospel but before his exile to Patmos. No specific recipients are identified, suggesting that the letter may have been intended for circulation among a number of churches in the province of Asia.

One particular heresy in the early Church was Gnosticism. "Its central teaching was that spirit is entirely good and matter is entirely evil."[45] As a consequence of this central teaching, Gnostics taught that salvation was achieved not through faith in Jesus, but through a special knowledge that man needed to attain. Although John does not specifically address Gnosticism in this letter, he decries false teachers and assures the believers of their salvation through Christ.

2 John

2 John was also written by the apostle John. As with 1 John, the author does not specifically identify himself in the letter other than to call himself "the elder." However, the style, content, and phrasing of this letter are all very similar to the Gospel of John and to 1 John. It was likely written at the same time as 1 John, between A.D. 85 and 95. This brief letter encourages the believers to practice discretion when showing hospitality to traveling teachers and preachers. John equates showing hospitality to false teachers as "sharing in [their] wicked work" (2 John 11).

---

[45] Hoerber, *Self-Study Bible*, 1925.

3 John

3 John was also written by the apostle John. As in 2 John, the author identifies himself as "the elder." It was likely written at the same time as 1 and 2 John, between A.D. 85 and 95. The letter is written to Gaius, a Christian in one of the churches in the province of Asia. John writes to praise Gaius for his faith and the hospitality he has shown to traveling missionaries. He also sharply rebukes Diotrephes, a church leader who "refuses to welcome the brothers" (3 John 10). Believers of every age should strive to follow the example of Gaius and support those charged with preaching the Word.

Jude

The author of this letter is Jude, another form of the Greek name Judas. The most likely author is Judas the half-brother of Jesus. The author identifies himself as "the brother of James," which he would only do if James (also the half-brother of Jesus, likely the author of the book of James, and a leader in the church at Jerusalem) was well-known among his recipients. Jude is somewhat similar in content to 2 Peter, suggesting that Peter may have borrowed from this letter. The recipients of the letter are not specified and could be either Jewish or Gentile Christians.

Although Jude desired to write about "the salvation we share" (Jude 3), he felt the need to instead combat false teachers which were plaguing the church. "Apparently these false teachers were trying to convince believers that being saved by grace gave them license to sin since their sins would no longer be held against them."[46] He calls on his readers to persevere in the midst of such false teachings and to "build yourselves up in your most holy faith" (Jude 20).

Revelation

The author of this letter identifies himself as John, most likely the apostle John. It was written at the beginning of a time of persecution for Christians. There are two possible dates for the book: during the reign of Nero (A.D. 54-68) or of Dominitian (A.D. 81-96). Most scholars favor a later date of writing, likely A.D. 95.

---

[46] Hoerber, *Self-Study Bible*, 1938.

■ The Books of the Bible

Revelation is *apocalyptic* in nature: writing that includes dreams or visions, unusual symbolic imagery, number symbolism, and a focus on events of the end times. It is a series of seven visions, each depicting the period of time from Jesus' ascension to his return on Judgment Day. The figurative language in Revelation is open to interpretation, but its central message is clear: God is in control and will ultimately triumph over Satan and the powers of evil. Revelation tells of God's "glory, wisdom, power, authority, righteous wrath and return to judge the world and to receive all who believe through God's grace into eternal bliss—into a new heaven, a new Jerusalem with the angelic hosts."[47]

---

[47] Hoerber, *Self-Study Bible,* 1942.

References

Baumler, Gary, and Kermit Moldenhauer, editors. *Christian Worship: Manual.* Northwestern Publishing House, 2002.

Hoerber, Robert G, editor. *Concordia Self-Study Bible: New International Version.* Concordia Publishing House, 1986.

Lewis, C.S. *Letters to Malcolm: Chiefly on Prayer.* Harcourt, Inc, 1964.

Maschke, Timothy H. *Gathered Guests: A Guide to Worship in the Lutheran Church.* Concordia Publishing House, 2009.

Schroeder, Jonathan E. *Planning Christian Worship (Supplemental Lectionary) – Year A.* Authorized by the Commission on Worship of the Wisconsin Evangelical Lutheran Synod.

Schroeder, Jonathan E., editor, and Daniel M. Deutschlander. *Planning Christian Worship (Supplemental Lectionary) – Year B – Festival Half.* Authorized by the Commission on Worship of the Wisconsin Evangelical Lutheran Synod.

www.ingramcontent.com/pod-product-compliance
Lightning Source LLC
Chambersburg PA
CBHW072109290426
44110CB00014B/1881